To: Madeleine

Happy Birthday

Brian & Marilyn

NEWFOUNDLAND AND LABRADOR

SOUVENIR BOOK

BRIAN C. BURSEY

Printed and bound in Canada by Friesen Printers.

ISBN 1-55056-526-5

Cover: *Fogo, as viewed from Bleak House. Two harbours, and a proximity to rich cod and seal resources, led to the development of Fogo as a major fishing and commercial centre. One of the oldest settlements on the northeast coast, Fogo had a sizeable permanent population by the early 1700s.*

Right: *The Spout. This prominent landmark, located midway between Bay Bulls and Petty Harbour, occurs when waves in a nearby sea cave force salt water and mist from a vent in the bedrock. During heavy swells, the 'Spout' can be seen for many miles out to sea.*

◄ Cape Race. One of the most powerful in the world, this lighthouse was built in 1907 as a beacon for trans-Atlantic shipping.

Iceberg at St. John's. Most Newfoundland and Labrador icebergs originate from glaciers on the west coast of Greenland. This iceberg, which towers approximately 50 metres above the water, is larger than most. Seven-eighths of its bulk remain underwater.

▶ Lighthouse at Redmonds Head, Bell Island.

Bowring Park, St. John's.

Headstone at Adams Cove, Conception Bay.

Mushrooms.

◄ Blueberries

Grandys Brook, southwestern Newfoundland.

Trinity, one of Newfoundland's most
historic communities.

Sandy Cove. This sandy beach is one of
several on the Eastport Peninsula.

► Natural arch, near Ochre Pit Cove, Conception Bay.

Wild flowers.

► Frozen waterfall, Northwest River, near Port Blandford.

Frozen mist, La Manche River.

◄ Late September, Terra Nova National Park.

White water lilies, Cocoanut Waters, Avalon Peninsula.

► St. Luke's Anglican Church (1895),
Newtown, Bonavista Bay.

Autumn morning, St. Alban's, Bay d'Espoir.

► Fall colours.

Stag Caribou.

◄ Rose Blanche. The name Rose Blanche is thought to be a corruption of the French 'roche blanche', or white rock. There are numerous outcroppings of white granite in the area.

Red Admiral Butterfly.

Thunder Brook, near Grand Falls.

Moose. Native to Labrador, this non-indigenous species was first introduced to the Island in 1878.

Iceberg, Conception Bay.

◄ Sea stack, Bell Island, Newfoundland.

English Harbour West.

◄ Fishing Boats at Frenchman's Cove, Bay of
Islands.

The Arches Public Beach, south of Daniel's
Harbour. Sightseers walking nearby provide
scale to these large, sea-carved arches.

► Glacial fiord, Gros Morne National Park.

Leaves of the red maple.

Spring canoeing on the Northwest Gander River.

Sunrise at Northwest Arm, Trinity Bay.

◄ Shipwreck at Blue Beach, St. Lawrence.

◄ Gypsum cliffs along Romaines Brook, near
Stephenville.

Fishing boat at Isle aux Morts.

The Tablelands, Gros Morne National Park. This area owes its distinct colouration to peridotite, a rusty brown rock which is toxic to most forms of vegetation. Peridotite, formed deep within the earth's crust, has been forced to the surface in western Newfoundland through 'plate tectonics' or the collision of the vast continental plates which make up the earth's crust. This unusual exposure was a prime reason for the designation of the Gros Morne area as a World Heritage Site by UNESCO.

► The Pitcher Plant, floral emblem of Newfoundland and Labrador.

Sagona, a resettled fishing community in Fortune Bay.

A summer evening on the Kenamu River, Labrador.

Lighthouse at Cape Bonavista, the traditional landfall of John Cabot. This lighthouse, erected in 1843, contains 200 year old lights which had been previously installed on Scotland's Inch Cape Rock.

Henley Harbour, Labrador.

Winter tilt in Labrador. Tilts serve as bases
for trapping and hunting, and for catching
trout and smelt through the ice.

Late winter near Kenemich, Labrador.

Common Puffin. Since puffins nest in burrows dug into soft turf, they are vulnerable to a variety of predators. Nesting on islands helps to reduce this threat.

Bakeapples. Called cloudberries elsewhere, bakeapples are found throughout Newfoundland and Labrador.

Polar Bear. Polar bears are relatively common in northern Labrador throughout the year, and are found as far south as St. John's in spring and early summer.

Minke Whale near Packs Harbour, Labrador. These medium-sized whales can be found close to shore where they feed on capelin, herring and mackerel. Mature minke whales, which are often referred to as 'grampus', average eight metres in length.

Inuit ruins at North Arm, Torngat Mountains, Labrador.

Ermine, northern Labrador.

◄ Churchill Falls. At 75 metres, Churchill
Falls is substantially higher than Niagara
Falls and one of the continent's largest
cataracts. Originally called Grand Falls,
and later Hamilton Falls, it was known
only to native people until visited by John
McLean of the Hudson's Bay Company in
1839. Water to the falls was largely
diverted in the late 1960s for development
of a 7,000,000 hp hydro-electric complex,
Canada's largest construction project to
that time.